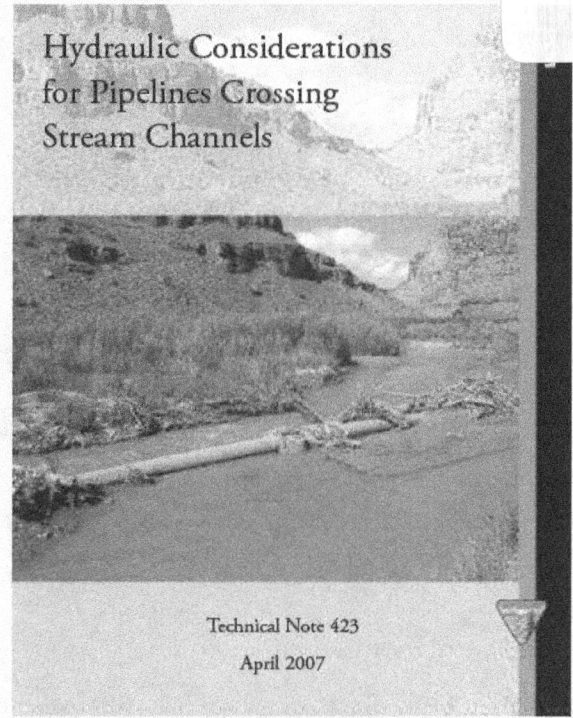

Hydraulic Considerations
for Pipelines Crossing
Stream Channels

Technical Note 423
April 2007

Hydraulic Considerations for Pipelines Crossing Stream Channels

Technical Note 423

By:

Jim Fogg
Surface Water Hydrologist
Bureau of Land Management
Denver, CO

and

Heidi Hadley
Salinity Coordinator
Bureau of Land Management
Salt Lake City, UT

2007

Contents

Abstract

High flow events have the potential to damage pipelines that cross stream channels, possibly contaminating runoff. A hydrologic analysis conducted during the design of the pipeline can help determine proper placement. Flood frequency and magnitude evaluations are required for pipelines that cross at the surface. There are several methods that can be used, including reconnaissance, physiographic, analytical, and detailed methods. The method used must be appropriate for the site's characteristics and the objectives of the analysis. Channel degradation and scour evaluations are required for pipelines crossing below the surface. Proper analysis and design can prevent future pipeline damage and reduce repair and replacement costs.

Introduction

In 2002, the U.S. Fish and Wildlife Service raised concerns about the potential for flash floods in ephemeral stream channels to rupture natural-gas pipelines and carry toxic condensates to the Green River, which would have deleterious effects on numerous special-status fish species (Figure 1). In November of the same year, BLM hydrologists visited the Uinta Basin in Utah to survey stream channels and compute flood magnitudes and depths to better understand possible flooding scenarios. From this they developed construction guidance for pipelines crossing streams in Utah. This guidance was later modified so that it was generally applicable to the arid and semiarid lands of the intermountain west. It may also have general applicability in other areas of the western United States. The purpose of this document is to present the modified guidance for placement of pipelines crossing above or below the surface of stream channels to prevent inundation or exposure of the pipe to the hydraulic forces of flood events.

Figure 1. Pipeline breaks during flooding can release condensate toxic to sensitive fish species.

Surface Crossings

Pipelines that cross stream channels on the surface should be located above all possible floodflows that may occur at the site. At a minimum, pipelines must be located above the 100-year flood elevation and preferably above the 500-year flood elevation. Two sets of relationships are available for estimating flood frequencies at ungaged sites in Utah. Thomas and Lindskov (1983) use drainage basin area and mean basin elevation for flood estimates for six Utah regions stratified by location and basin elevation (Table 1). Thomas et al. (1997) also use drainage area and mean basin elevation to estimate magnitude and frequency of floods throughout the southwestern U.S., including seven regions that cover the entire State of Utah. Results from both sets of equations should be examined to estimate the 100- and 500-year floods, since either of the relations may provide questionable results if the pipeline crosses a stream near the boundary of a flood region or if the drainage area or mean basin elevation for the crossing exceed the limits of the data set used to develop the equations.

Table 1. Examples of flood frequency equations for ungaged sites in Utah.

Regression equations for peak discharges for Uinta Basin (from Thomas and Lindskov 1983)			
Discharge $\underline{Q}$ in cubic feet per second, $\underline{A}$rea in square miles, $\underline{E}$levation in thousands of feet			
Recurrence interval (yrs)	Equation	Number of stations used in analysis	Average standard error of estimate (%)
2	$Q = 1{,}500 \, A^{0.403} \, E^{-1.90}$	25	82
5	$Q = 143{,}000 \, A^{0.374} \, E^{3.66}$	25	66
10	$Q = 1.28 \times 10^6 \, A^{0.362} \, E^{4.50}$	25	64
25	$Q = 1.16 \times 10^7 \, A^{0.352} \, E^{5.32}$	25	66
50	$Q = 4.47 \times 10^7 \, A^{0.347} \, E^{5.85}$	25	70
100	$Q = 1.45 \times 10^8 \, A^{0.343} \, E^{6.29}$	25	74

Procedures for estimating 100-year and 500-year flood magnitudes for other States are described in the U.S. Geological Survey's National Flood Frequency Program (Ries and Crouse 2002) (Figure 2). Full documentation of the equations and information necessary to solve them is provided in individual reports for each State. The National Flood Frequency (NFF) Website (*http://water. usgs.gov/software/nff.html*) provides State summaries of the equations in NFF, links to online reports for many States, and factsheets summarizing reports for States with new or corrected equations. Background information in each State's flood frequency reports should be checked to ensure that application of the equations is not attempted for sites with independent variables outside the range used to develop the predictive equations.

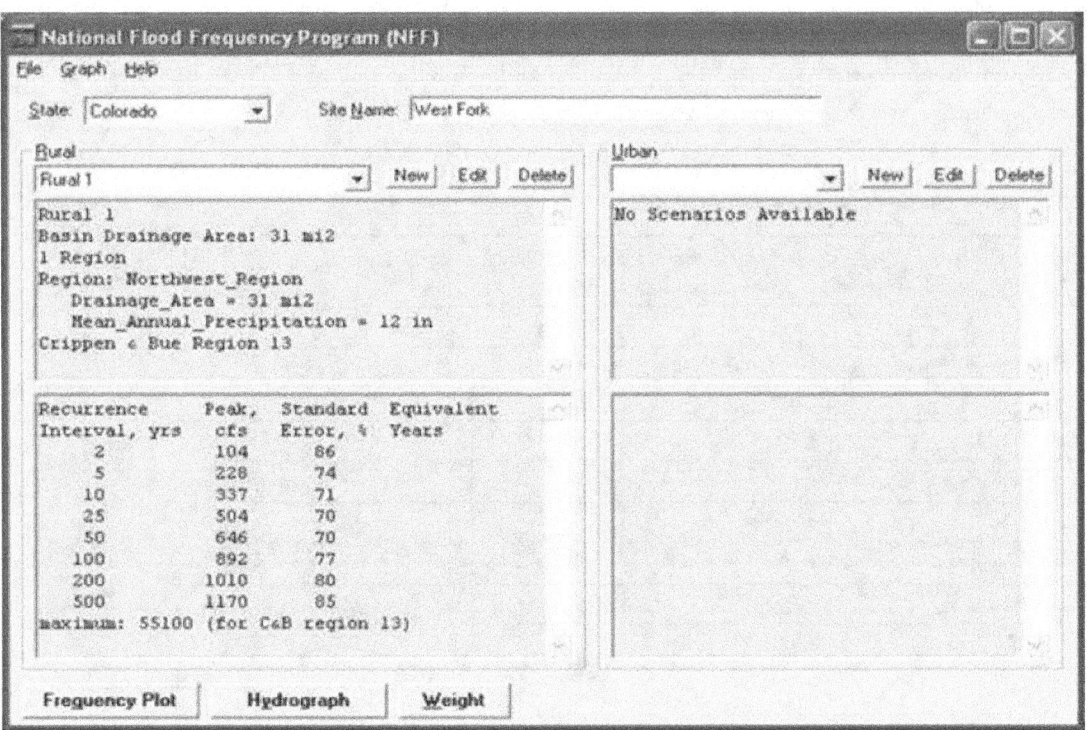

Figure 2. View of the output from NFF.

Once the flood frequency for a site has been estimated, determining the depth of flow associated with an extreme flood (i.e., the elevation of the pipeline at the crossing) may be approached in a number of ways. Procedures for estimating depth of flow for extreme floods in Utah are presented in Thomas and Lindskov (1983). Similar procedures presented in Burkham (1977, 1988) are generally applicable for locations throughout the Great Basin and elsewhere. The reconnaissance, physiographic, analytical, and detailed methods described in those reports will be summarized briefly in this paper. Burkham (1988) describes an additional method (historical method) not presented here, since the data for its use (high-water marks for an extreme historical flood with known discharge and recurrence interval) are rarely available in public land situations for which this guidance is intended.

Reconnaissance Method

The reconnaissance method (as the name implies) is a fairly rough and imprecise method for delineating flood-prone areas (Burkham 1988; Thomas and Lindskov 1983). It is most applicable to stable or degrading alluvial channels with multiple terrace surfaces, although such terraces may be difficult to detect on severely degrading streams. In this procedure, the channel of interest is examined to approximate the area that would be inundated by a large flood. A geomorphic reconnaissance of the site is conducted, and it may be supplemented with aerial photos, maps, and historical information available for the reach of interest. In addition to the morphology of the channel, floodplain, and terraces, information on vegetation (e.g., species, flood tolerance, drought tolerance) and soils (e.g., development, stratification, and drainage) can be helpful for identifying flood-prone areas (Burkham 1988). For best results, the geomorphic analysis should include reaches upstream and downstream of the site and should attempt to determine the general state of the stream channel as aggrading, degrading, or stable. (Additional guidance on detection of stream degradation is presented in the section on subsurface crossings).

In the reconnaissance method, identification of bankfull elevation and the active floodplain (i.e., floodplain formed by the present flow regime) provides **inadequate** conveyance information for extreme flood events (Figure 3). Past floodplains or present terraces also must be identified, since these surfaces may be inundated by extreme floods in the present flow regime, especially in arid and semiarid environments. Pipelines should be constructed so that they cross at or above the elevation of the highest and outermost terrace (Figure 4). The highest terrace is unlikely to be accessed in the modern flow regime by any but the most extreme floods.

Figure 3. Although this pipeline crossed above the bankfull channel indicators, it was not high enough to escape more extreme floods.

Figure 4. This New Mexico pipeline crosses the channel near the elevation of the highest terrace, which places it above even the most extreme flood events.

Practitioners of the reconnaissance method need considerable experience in geomorphology, sedimentation, hydraulics, soil science, and botany. Also, since this method is based on a geomorphic reconnaissance of the site, no flood frequency analysis is required and no recurrence interval can be assigned to the design elevation. An additional drawback to the method is that the accuracy of the results is unknown. However, the reconnaissance method may be the most rational one for delineating flood-prone areas on some alluvial fans and valley floors where channels become discontinuous (Burkham 1988). While this is the quickest approach to designing a stream crossing, it likely will result in the most conservative estimate (i.e., highest elevation and greatest construction cost) for suspension of the pipeline.

Physiographic Method

A slightly more intensive approach to designing a stream crossing is based on the physiographic method for estimating flood depths at ungaged sites described by Thomas and Lindskov (1983) and Burkham (1988). The procedure uses regional regression equations (similar to the flood frequency equations described above) to estimate **maximum** depth of flow associated with a specified recurrence-interval flood (Table 2). Flood depth is then added to a longitudinal survey of the channel **thalweg** in the vicinity of the crossing (10 to 20 channel widths in length), resulting in a longitudinal profile of the specified flood. Elevation of the flood profile at the point of pipeline crossing is the elevation above which the pipeline must be suspended. The method is generally applicable where 1) the project site is physiographically similar to the drainage basins used to develop the regression equations and 2) soil characteristics are the same at the project site as in the basins where the regression equations were developed. While this procedure requires a field survey and calculation of flood depths at points along the channel, it may result in a lower crossing elevation (and possibly lower costs) for the pipeline. Also, since the regional regression equations estimate flood depths for specific recurrence-interval floods, it is possible to place a recurrence interval on the crossing design for risk calculations. However, regional regression equations linking depth of flood to recurrence interval have not been developed for many areas. In States where they have been developed (e.g., Alabama, Colorado, Illinois, Kansas, and Oklahoma), standard errors of the estimates have ranged from 17 to 28 percent, with an average standard error of 23 percent (Burkham 1988).

Table 2. Examples of depth frequency equations for ungaged sites in Utah.

Regression equations for flood depths for Uinta Basin (from Thomas and Lindskov 1983)			
Flood depth D in feet, Area in square miles, Elevation in thousands of feet			
Recurrence interval (yrs)	Equation	Number of stations used in analysis	Average standard error of estimate (%)
2	$D = 1.03 \, A^{0.159}$	16	30
5	$D = 13.3 \, A^{0.148} E^{-1.03}$	16	28
10	$D = 68.6 \, A^{0.131} E^{-1.69}$	16	26
25	$D = 556 \, A^{0.128} E^{-2.59}$	16	24
50	$D = 1330 \, A^{0.123} E^{-2.95}$	15	24
100	$D = 1210 \, A^{0.130} E^{-2.86}$	14	22

Analytical Method

The analytical method described by Burkham (1988) uses uniform flow equations to estimate depth of flow associated with a particular magnitude and frequency of discharge. Typically, a trial-and-error procedure is used to solve the Manning uniform flow equation for depth of flow, given a design discharge (i.e., a flood of specified recurrence interval), a field-surveyed cross section and channel slope, and an estimate of the Manning roughness coefficient (n). Numerous software packages are available to facilitate the trial-and-error solution procedure (e.g., WinXSPRO). Since the Manning formula is linear with respect to the roughness coefficient, estimating this coefficient can be a significant source of error and is likely the most significant weakness in this approach. Estimating roughness coefficients (n values) for ungaged sites is a matter of engineering judgment, but n values typically are a function of slope, depth of flow, bed-material particle size, and bedforms present during the passage of the flood wave. Guidance is available in many hydraulic references (e.g., Chow 1959). Selecting n values for flows above the bankfull stage is particularly difficult, since vegetation plays a major role in determining resistance to flow. Barnes (1967) presents photographic examples of field-verified n values, and Arcement and Schneider (1989) present comprehensive guidance for calculating n values for both channels and vegetated overbank areas (i.e., floodplains). Depth of flow determined with uniform flow equations, such as the Manning equation, represents **mean** depth of flow to be added to the **cross section** at the site of the pipeline crossing.

Burkham (1977, 1988) also presented a simplified technique for estimating depth of flow, making use of the general equation for the depth-discharge relation:

$$d = C \, Q^{f}$$

Values of f (the slope of the relationship when plotted on logarithmic graph paper) can be determined from "at-station" hydraulic geometry relationships at gaging stations in the region. Only the upper portion of the gaging-station ratings should be used to derive the slope (f value) for application to extreme floods, since a substantial portion of the flow may be conveyed in the overbank area. Alternatively, Burkham (1977, 1988) presents a simplified procedure for estimating f that requires only a factor for channel shape. Leopold and Langbein (1962) computed a theoretical value of 0.42 for natural channels, while Burkham (1988) computed a theoretical value of 0.46 for parabolic cross sections. Burkham (1977) earlier reported an average f value of 0.42 from 539 gaging stations scattered along the eastern seaboard and upper Midwest, while Leopold and Maddock (1953) reported an average f value of 0.40 for 20 river cross sections in the Great Plains and the Southwest. Park (1977) summarized f values from 139 sites around the world and found most values occurred in the range of 0.3 to 0.4. Additional assumptions in Burkham (1977, 1988) enable an estimate of the coefficient C in the depth-discharge relationship with only a single field measurement of width and maximum depth at some reference level in the channel (e.g., bankfull stage)

(Burkham 1977, 1988). Depth of flow determined from Burkham's simplified technique represents **maximum** depth of flow to be added to the **thalweg** at the cross section.

The analytical methods described by Burkham (1977, 1988) generally will be more accurate than the physiographic and reconnaissance methods described previously; thus, they may result in lower pipeline elevations and construction costs than the previous methods. However, analysis of flood elevations for the most sensitive situations should probably be conducted with the detailed method described below.

Detailed Method

Additional savings in construction costs for pipelines crossing channels may be realized by applying a detailed water-surface-profile model of flow through the crossing site. The water-surface-profile model requires a detailed survey of both the longitudinal channel profile (at least 20 channel widths in length) and several cross sections along the stream (Figure 5). Design flows (e.g., 100-year

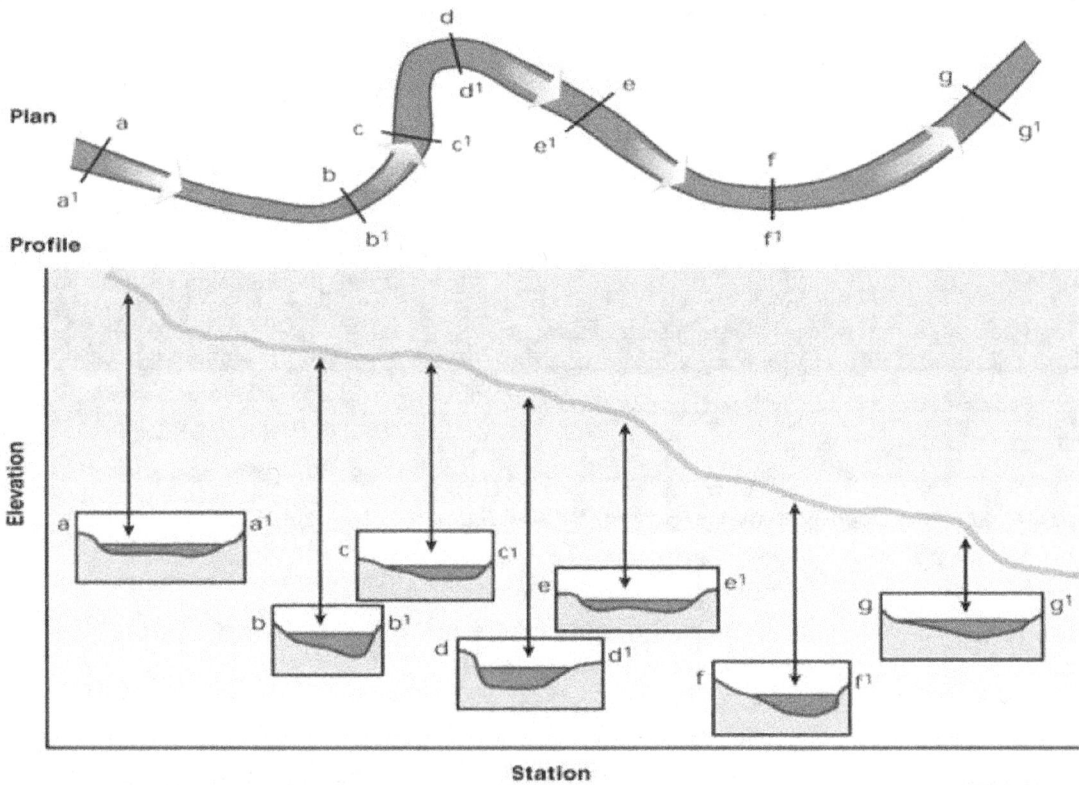

Figure 5. Application of a water-surface-profile model requires both a longitudinal channel profile and several surveyed cross sections (Federal Interagency Stream Restoration Working Group 1998).

and 500-year floods) are calculated for the channel at the crossing with the regional regression equations described above and routed through the surveyed channel reach using a step-backwater analysis. The step-backwater analysis uses the principles of conservation of mass and conservation of energy to calculate water-surface elevations at each surveyed cross section. Computed water-surface elevations at successive cross sections are linked to provide a water-surface profile for the flood of interest through the reach of interest. The computations are routinely accomplished in standard software, such as the U.S. Army Corps of Engineers' HEC-RAS model. Whereas the analytical methods described previously assume steady, uniform flow conditions through the reach, a detailed water-surface-profile model is capable of handling both gradually and (to some extent) rapidly varied flow conditions. Since the computation uses a detailed channel survey, it is the most accurate method to use; however, it is likely the most expensive method for the same reason. Burkham (1988) indicates that the error in flood depths predicted from step-backwater analysis can be expected to be less than 20 percent. The step-backwater computations require an estimate of the Manning roughness coefficient (n) as an indicator of resistance to flow and assume fairly stable channel boundaries. Estimation of the roughness coefficient

(n) includes the same considerations discussed previously for the analytical methods. The assumption of fairly stable channel boundaries is not always met with sand-bed channels and is an issue of considerable importance for designing subsurface pipeline crossings as well.

Of the methods presented for determining elevation of floods for pipelines crossing channels, the detailed method is the most accurate and should be used for situations with high resource values, infrastructure investment, construction costs, or liabilities in downstream areas. In undeveloped areas, the physiographic and analytical methods may be used to provide quick estimates of flood elevations for sites with fewer downstream concerns. The reconnaissance method provides the roughest estimates but may be all that is warranted in very unstable areas, such as alluvial fans or low relief valley floors (e.g., near playas). The detailed, analytical, and physiographic methods all assume relatively stable channel boundaries but may be used on sand channels with an accompanying loss of accuracy. In very sandy channels, the accuracy of results from the detailed method may not be significantly better than the results from one of the intermediate methods unless a mobile-boundary model is used (Burkham 1988).

Subsurface (Buried) Crossings

Since many of the pipelines are small and most of the channels are ephemeral, it is commonplace to bury the pipelines rather than suspending them above the streams. The practice of burying pipelines at channel crossings likely is both cheaper and easier than suspending them above all floodflows; however, an analysis of channel degradation and scour should be completed to ensure the pipelines are not exposed and broken during extreme runoff events (Figure 6). Without such an analysis, channels should be excavated to bedrock and pipelines placed beneath all alluvial material.

Figure 6. Channel degradation or scour during flash-flood events may expose buried pipelines, resulting in costly breaks.

Buried pipelines may be exposed by streambed lowering resulting from channel degradation, channel scour, or a combination of the two. Channel degradation occurs over a long stream reach or even the entire drainage network and is generally associated with the overall lowering of the landscape. Degradation also may be associated with changes in upstream watershed or channel conditions that alter the water and sediment yield of the basin. Channel scour is a local phenomenon associated with passage of one or more flood events or site-specific hydraulic conditions that may be natural or human-caused in origin. Either process can expose buried pipelines to excessive forces associated with extreme flow events, and an analysis of each is required to ensure integrity of the crossing.

Channel Degradation

Detection of long-term channel degradation must be attempted, even if there is no indication of local scour. Conceptual models of channel evolution (e.g., Simon 1989) have been proposed to describe a more-or-less predictable sequence of channel changes that a stream undergoes in response to disturbance in the channel or the watershed. Many of these models are based on a "space for time" substitution, whereby downstream conditions are interpreted as preceding (in time) the immediate location of interest, and upstream conditions are interpreted as following (in time) the immediate location of interest. Thus, a reach in the middle of the watershed that previously looked like the channel upstream will evolve to look like the channel downstream (Federal Interagency Stream Restoration Working Group 1998). Since channel evolution models can help predict current trends where a pipeline crosses a channel, they may indicate areas to be avoided when relocation of the crossing is an option. Most conceptual models of channel evolution have been developed for landscapes dominated by streams with cohesive banks; however, the same processes occur in streams with noncohesive banks, with somewhat less well-defined stages.

Geomorphic indicators of recent channel incision (e.g., obligate and facultative riparian species on present-day stream terraces elevated above the water table) also may be helpful for diagnosing channel conditions. However, long-term trends in channel evolution are often reversed during major flood events, especially for intermittent and ephemeral channels in arid and semiarid environments. Thus, a stream that is degrading during annual and intermediate flood events may be filled with sediment (i.e., it may aggrade) from tributary inputs during a major flood, and channels that are associated with sediment storage (i.e., aggrading) during the majority of runoff events may be "blown out" with major degradation during unusual and extreme large floods.

In some situations, a quantitative analysis of channel degradation may be warranted. Plots of streambed elevation against time permit evaluation of bed-level adjustment and indicate whether a major phase of channel incision has passed or is ongoing. However, comparative channel survey data are rarely available for the proposed location for a pipeline to cross a channel. In instances where a gaging station is operated at or near the crossing, it is usually possible to determine long-term aggradation or degradation by plotting the change in stage through time for one or more selected discharges. The procedure is called a specific-gage analysis (Figure 7) and is described in detail in *Stream Corridor Restoration: Principles, Processes, and Practices* (Federal Interagency Stream Restoration Working Group 1998). When there is no gaging station near the proposed channel crossing, nearby locations on the same stream or in the same river basin may provide a regional perspective on long-term channel adjustments. However, specific-gage records indicate only the conditions in the vicinity of the particular gaging station and do not necessarily reflect river response farther upstream or downstream of the gage. Therefore, it is advisable to investigate other data in order to make predictions about potential channel degradation at a site.

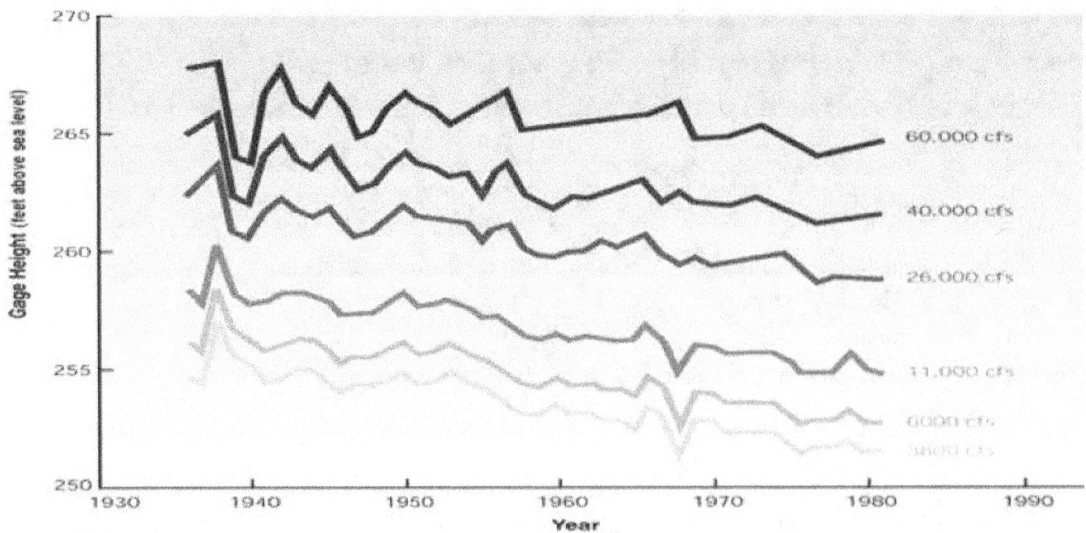

Figure 7. Specific-gage plots of the gage heights associated with index flows through time may indicate general channel lowering in the drainage basin (adapted from Federal Interagency Stream Restoration Working Group 1998; Biedenharn et al. 1997).

Other sources of information include the biannual bridge inspection reports required in all States for bridge maintenance. In most States, these reports include channel cross sections or bed elevations under the bridge, and a procedure similar to specific gage analysis may be attempted (Figure 8). Simon (1989, 1992) presents mathematical functions for describing bed-level adjustments through time, fitting elevation data at a site to either a power function or an exponential function of time. Successive cross sections from a series of bridges in a basin also may be used to construct a longitudinal profile of the channel network; sequential profiles so constructed may be used to document channel adjustments through time (Figure 9). Again, bridge inspection reports so used indicate only the conditions in the vicinity of those particular bridges (where local scour may be present) and must be interpreted judiciously for sites upstream, downstream, or between the bridges used in the analysis.

In the absence of channel surveys, gaging stations, and bridge inspection reports (or other records of structural repairs along a channel), it may be necessary to investigate channel aggradation and degradation using quantitative techniques described in Richardson et al. (2001) and Lagasse et al. (2001). Techniques for assessing vertical stability of the channel include incipient motion analysis, analysis of armoring potential, equilibrium slope analysis, and sediment continuity analysis. Incipient motion analysis and analysis of armoring potential are equally applicable to

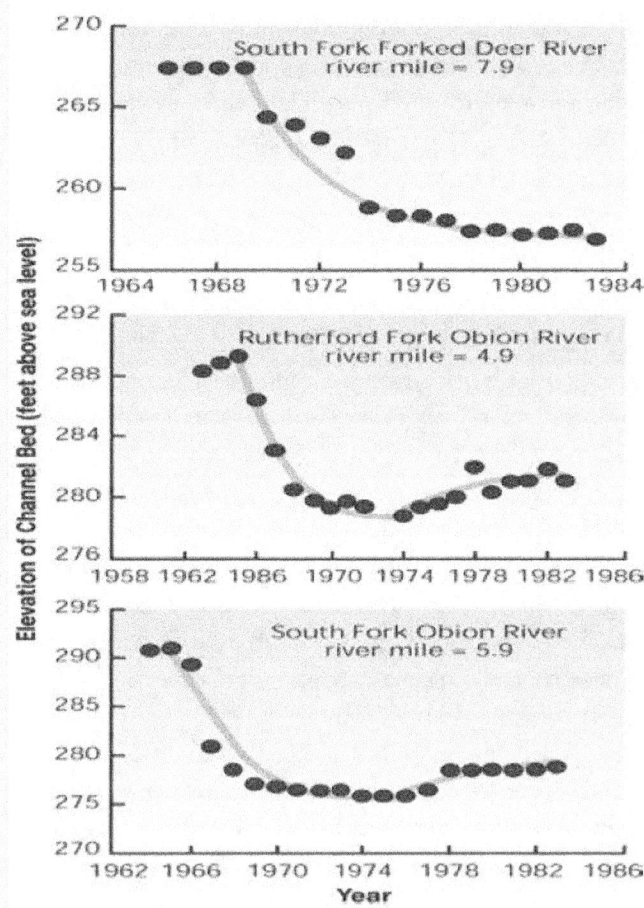

Figure 8. Plots of bed elevation versus time may be developed from biannual bridge inspection reports to document systemwide degradation or aggradation (Federal Interagency Stream Restoration Working Group 1998).

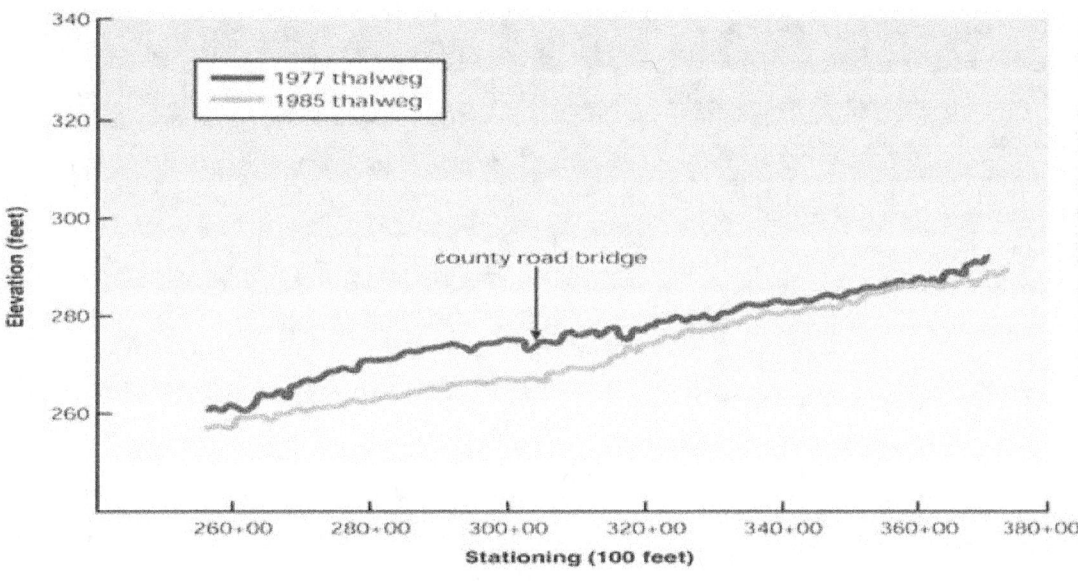

Figure 9. Sequential longitudinal profiles also may be used to document channel lowering through time (Federal Interagency Stream Restoration Working Group 1988; Biedenharn et al. 1997).

both long-term degradation and short-term scour and fill processes, while equilibrium-slope and sediment-continuity analyses are more closely tied to long-term channel processes (i.e., degradation and aggradation).

Channel Scour

In addition to long-term channel degradation at subsurface crossings, general channel scour must be addressed to ensure safety of the pipeline. General scour is different from long-term degradation in that general scour may be cyclic or related to the passing of a flood (Richardson and Davis 2001). Channel scour and fill processes occur naturally along a given channel, and both reflect the redistribution of sediment and short-term adjustments that enable the channel to maintain a quasi-equilibrium form. In other words, channels in dynamic equilibrium experience various depths of scour during the rising stages of a flood that frequently correspond to equal amounts of fill during the falling stages, resulting in minimal changes in channel-bed elevation. Where pipelines cross channels, it is important to determine the potential maximum depth of scour so that the pipeline is buried to a sufficient depth and does not become exposed when bed scour occurs during a flood.

General scour occurs when sediment transport through a stream reach is greater than the sediment load being supplied from upstream and is usually associated with changes in the channel cross section. General scour can occur in natural channels wherever a pipeline crosses a constriction in the channel cross section (contraction scour). Equations for calculating contraction scour generally fall into two categories, depending on the inflow of bed-material sediment from upstream. In situations where there is little to no bed-material transport from upstream (generally coarse-bed streams with gravel and larger bed materials), contraction scour should be estimated using clear-water scour equations. In situations where there is considerable bed-material transport into the constricted section (i.e., for most sand-bed streams), contraction scour should be estimated using live-bed scour equations. Live-bed and clear-water scour equations can be found in many hydraulic references (e.g., Richardson and Davis 2001). In either case, estimates of general scour in the vicinity of

the pipeline crossing must be added to the assessment of channel degradation for estimating the depth of burial for the crossing.

Other components of general scour can result from placement of subsurface crossings relative to the alignment of the stream channel. Pipelines crossing at bends in the channel are particularly troublesome, since bends are naturally unstable and tend to collect both ice and debris (which can cause additional constrictions in the flow). Channel-bottom elevations are usually lower on the outside of meander bends and may be more than twice as deep as the average depth in straighter portions of the channel. Crossings in the vicinity of stream confluences also create difficulties, since flood stages and hydraulic forces may be strongly influenced by backwater conditions at the downstream confluence. For example, sediment deposits from tributary inputs may induce contraction scour opposite or downstream of the deposit. Additional complications are introduced where pipelines are located near other obstructions in the channel. Channel-spanning obstructions (e.g., beaver dams or large wood) may induce plunge-pool scour downstream of the structure, and individual obstructions in the channel induce local scour akin to pier scour characteristic of bridge piers at highway crossings.

Even in the absence of contraction scour, general scour will still occur in most sand-bed channels during the passage of major floods. Since sand is easily eroded and transported, interaction between the flow of water and the sand bed results in different configurations of the stream bed with varying conditions of flow. The average height of dune bedforms is roughly one-third to one-half the mean flow depth, and the maximum height of dunes may nearly equal the mean flow depth. Thus, if the mean depth of flow in a channel was 5 feet, maximum dune height could also approach 5 feet, half of which would be below the mean elevation of the stream bed (Lagasse et al. 2001). Similarly, Simons, Li, and Associates (1982) present equations for antidune height as a function of mean velocity, but limit maximum antidune height to mean flow depth. Consequently, formation of antidunes during high flows not only increases mean water-surface elevation by one-half the wave height, it also reduces the mean bed elevation by one-half the wave height. Richardson and Davis (2001) reported maximum general scour of one to two times the average flow depth where two channels come together in a braided stream.

Pipeline crossings that are buried rather than suspended above all major flow events should address all of the components of degradation, scour, and channel-lowering due to bedforms described above. In addition, once a determination is made on how deep to bury the pipeline at the stream crossing, the elevation of the pipe should be held constant across the floodplain. If the line is placed at shallower depths beneath the floodplain, channel migration may expose the line where it is not designed to pass beneath the channel (Figure 10).

Figure 10. Lateral migration of this stream channel during high water excavated a section of pipeline under the floodplain that was several feet shallower than at the original stream crossing.

In complex situations or where consequences of pipeline failure are significant, consideration should be given to modeling the mobile-bed hydraulics with a numerical model such as HEC-6 (U.S. Army Corps of Engineers 1993) or BRI-STARS (Molinas 1990). The Federal Interagency Stream Restoration Working Group (1998) summarizes the capabilities of these and other models and provides references for model operation and user guides where available.

Conclusion

Pipelines that cross perennial, intermittent, and ephemeral stream channels should be constructed to withstand floods of extreme magnitude to prevent rupture and accidental contamination of runoff during high flow events. Pipelines crossing at the surface must be constructed high enough to remain above the highest possible floodflows at each crossing, and pipelines crossing below the surface must be buried deep enough to remain undisturbed by scour and fill processes typically associated with passage of peak flows. A hydraulic analysis should be completed during the pipeline design phase to avoid repeated maintenance of such crossings and eliminate costly repairs and potential environmental degradation associated with pipeline breaks at stream crossings.

Literature Cited

Arcement, G.J., Jr. and V.R. Schneider. 1989. Guide for selecting Manning's roughness coefficients for natural channels and flood plains. U.S. Geological Survey Water-Supply Paper 2339. 38 pp.

Barnes, H.H., Jr. 1967. Roughness characteristics of natural channels. U.S. Geological Survey Water-Supply Paper 1849. 213 pp.

Biedenharn, D.S., C.M. Elliott, and C.C. Watson. 1997. The WES stream investigation and streambank stabilization handbook. Prepared for the U.S. Environmental Protection Agency by the U.S. Army Corps of Engineers Waterways Experiment Station. Vicksburg, MS.

Burkham, D.E. 1977. A technique for determining depths for T-year discharges in rigid boundary channels. U.S. Geological Survey Water-Resources Investigations 77-83. 38 pp.

Burkham, D.E. 1988. Methods for delineating flood-prone areas in the Great Basin of Nevada and adjacent states. U.S. Geological Survey Water-Supply Paper 2316. 20 pp.

Chow, V.T. 1959. Open-channel hydraulics. McGraw Hill, New York. 680 pp.

Federal Interagency Stream Restoration Working Group. 1998. Stream corridor restoration: Principles, processes, and practices. National Technical Information Service, Order No. PB98-158348INQ, Washington, DC.

Lagasse, P.F., J.D. Schall, and E.V. Richardson. 2001. Stream stability at highway structures. Hydraulic Engineering Circular No. 20, Third Edition, FHWA NHI 01-002. Federal Highway Administration, Washington, DC.

Leopold, L.B. and W.B. Langbein. 1962. The concept of entropy in landscape evolution. U.S. Geological Survey Professional Paper 500-A. 20 pp.

Leopold, L.B. and T. Maddock, Jr. 1953. The hydraulic geometry of stream channels and some physiographic implications. U.S. Geological Survey Professional Paper 252. 57 pp.

Molinas, A. 1990. Bridge stream tube model for alluvial river simulation (BRI-STARS), user's manual. National Cooperative Highway Research Program, Project No. HR 15-11. Transportation Research Board, Washington, DC.

Park, C.C. 1977. World-wide variations in hydraulic geometry exponents of stream channels: An analysis and some observations. Journal of Hydrology 33:133-146.

Richardson, E.V. and S.R. Davis. 2001. Evaluating scour at bridges. Hydraulic Engineering Circular No. 18, Fourth Edition, FHWA NHI 01-001. Federal Highway Administration, Washington, DC.

Richardson, E.V., D.B. Simons, and P.F. Lagasse. 2001. Highways in the river environment. Report FHWA NHI 01-004, Hydraulic Design Series No. 6. Federal Highway Administration, Washington, DC.

Ries, K.G., III and M.Y. Crouse. 2002. The National Flood Frequency Program, version 3: A computer program for estimating magnitude and frequency of floods for ungaged sites. U.S. Geological Survey Water-Resources Investigations Report 02-4168. 42 pp.

Simon, A. 1989. A model of channel response in distributed alluvial channels. Earth Surface Processes and Landforms 14(1): 11-26.

Simon, A. 1992. Energy, time and channel evolution in catastrophically disturbed fluvial systems. In Phillips, J.D. and W.H. Renwick (eds.). Geomorphic systems: geomorphology. Vol. 5. pp. 345-372.

Simons, Li, and Associates. 1982. Engineering analysis of fluvial systems. Fort Collins, CO.

Thomas, B.E. and K.L. Lindskov. 1983. Methods for estimating peak discharge and flood boundaries of stream in Utah. U.S. Geological Survey Water-Resources Investigations Report 83-4129. 77 pp.

Thomas, B.E., H.W. Hjalmarson, and S.D. Waltemeyer. 1997. Methods for estimating magnitude and frequency of floods in the southwestern United States. U.S. Geological Survey Water-Supply Paper 2433. 195 pp.

U.S. Army Corps of Engineers. 1993. HEC-6 scour and deposition in rivers and reservoirs: Users manual. Hydrologic Engineering Center, Davis, CA.